CW01003718

Skydive

Leaping from the Ledge: Aspects of Age
and Adolescence

Poems and stories

By

Andrew Brown

Stairwell Books

Published by Stairwell Books
70 Barbara Drive
Norwalk
CT 06851 USA

ISBN: 978-1-939269-04-1

Printed and bound in the UK by Russell Press

Layout and cover design: Alan Gillott
Cover Photograph: Aprilia Zank
Back cover inset photograph: Dennis Low

Table of Contents

Adolescence

A Spell in the Army

"This my friend, the old man
He fought in the war,
and he's proud of it.
And he can show you medals
to prove that he was brave"

So you see PE lessons ain't about runnin' round fields no more. Nah. All that's finished. Since we're all sixteen now an' about to leave anyway it's all about bundling in the school bus an' goin' down Dagenham Bowling Alley. It's quite a laugh really - 'cept last week when Droopy Bollocks dropped a friggin' bowling ball on me foot an' 'alf bleedin' crippled me.

But there's other stuff, too - like pretend RE lessons with Ronnie Biggs (well 'e ain't really - 'e's Mr Briggs - but we call 'im Ronnie). Suddenly 'e wants to know if we can get our 'ands on a petrol mower 'cause then 'we can go do someone some good' 'e says. 'Christianity in practice' 'e says. So we all of us end up down this old bloke's 'ouse in Corringham or Stanford-le-Hope or somewhere an' the poor old sod looks a bit worried, don't 'e? But we tell 'im it's okay - we've only come to cut 'is grass an' tidy up 'is garden. And it flippin' needs it, too. 'E's got this great big lawn an' it ain't been cut all year - eighteen inches 'igh it is···

'Come on, Nylon' Tony Pritchard says. 'Put yer back into it···'

'You can shut yer face' I says. Well, I mean, I couldn't even push it, could I? The grass gets all chewed up inside the mower an' it stops turning, don't it? So after a bit we worked out if you pushed the handle right down to ya shins like - an' lifted up the front end you could just about get through it without stoppin'. It killed yer back, mind. After ten minutes o' that I'd 'ad enough.

'I'm thirsty' I says an' Ronnie Biggs says Mr Lawns'll give us a drink.

'He's got squash if you want it' 'e says. 'And you can make him a cup of tea as well, Brian, while you're about it. And me' 'e says.

'Mr Lawns?' I says. I give 'im a bit of a look. 'You're 'avin' me on.' I says. ''E can't be called Mr Lawns⋯'

'That's his name⋯' 'e says. 'Bill Lawns. And mind you treat him with respect' 'e says. ''Cause his generation did their bit in the war and don't you forget it, lad.'

I knock on 'is door - an' I go in an' it's full of old stuff an' a bit whiffy like. An' there 'e is sitting there lookin' out the window.

''Ello' I says.

'How you getting' on?' 'e says. 'I can't do what I used to do' 'e says. 'Not at my age⋯' Well, lookin' at 'im I'm not surprised. I mean 'e looks a bit knackered like. 'I've been livin' in this house since 1946' 'e says. An' 'e starts ramblin' on don't 'e? 'Things ain't what they used to be' 'e says. Oh cripes - 'ere we go, I think to myself.

'1946' 'e says. ''Omes fit for 'eroes.'

'You what?' I says. He looks out the window an' an Eastern National bus pulls up at the bus stop.

'The Seventy-Two 'ad a puncture out there last week' 'e tells me.

'Did it?' I says.

'An' you see that damp patch over there by me dryer? That's been on the rise since the famous floods of 1953. I keep pointing it out to that man from the 'ousing - but 'e don't see it - 'e don't wanna know that's the point - it'd cost 'im too much flippin' money - an' 'e thinks I'll be dead soon⋯' I start lookin' round for the teapot. The old boy rambles on.

'You know them Germans - dropping all them bombs in the Blitz? Well, our RAF boys went back an' flattened the buggers, didn' they? - that sorted them - Dresden an' all that. I got medals you know? Rows

4

o' bloody medals - but what does that mean when you end ya days in a council 'ouse like this surrounded by a bloody jungle? What good's come out of all that, can you tell me that, my son?'

'I dunno' I says. 'Where'd you keep ya sugar?' But 'e don't answer.

'These wars are always 'just' you know. Oh yes. They always tell you you're fighting for your King or your Country or God or your Fellow Man or something. Nothin' never changes. The 'war to end war' they said - but we knew it wouldn't - you can't justify 'just' wars you know - 'cause it's always gonna end up badly for some poor bugger you can be certain o' that - an' it ain't never the rich is it? Oh no. It's never them what pays the price··· ''Omes fit for 'eroes! Just look at the bloody place' I 'and 'im 'is cup o' tea.

'Thanks' 'e says, an' suddenly the mower stops an' there's a load of shouting an' screamin' from outside.

'What's up?' I yell at Tony through the window.

'We've cut a snake in two' he says. He's kinda excited. 'Come out an' 'ave a look' 'e says. So I go out an' there's this thing with its guts 'anging out, cut clean in two - its little mouth open like it's surprised - an' a bit pigged off - that it's suddenly got filleted out of nowhere.

'What the 'ell is it?' someone asks.

'Well, it's not a boa constrictor is it?' I says. Ronnie Biggs comes up to 'ave a butchers.

'Poor thing' 'e says. 'It's not a grass snake - it's not the right colour - maybe it's a slow worm - what do you reckon, Brian, do you think it's a slow worm?'

'I've no idea, sir' I say. ''Ow should I know? But whatever it is, it ain't one no more.'

'Quite' says Ronnie, an' 'e changes the subject. 'What about that cup of tea you were making?'

5

Back inside, I 'ave to explain to Bill Lawns what's been goin' on. 'A snake' I says. 'Cut clean in 'alf···'

'Oh' 'e says as if 'e's not even sure what a snake is no more. 'There's always something what pays the price' 'e says. 'Always.' Suddenly 'e gives me a look like 'e's woken up out of a deep sleep. It kinda takes me by surprise. 'What're you gonna do with yourself?' 'e asks.

'What?' I says.

'Well, if this is your last year at school you're gonna have to look for work, aren't you - find yourself a trade···?' Suddenly I feel bad. To be honest, it's not something I wanna talk about or even think about. 'How old are you?' he says. 'Sixteen? Seventeen?'

'Thereabouts' I says.

'You ought to know at your age. I started work when I was thirteen' 'e says. 'E tells me the trouble with youth today is that none of us knows what we want. 'Too many opportunities' 'e says. 'Too much schooling··· You know what I reckon, my son?'

'What?' I says.

'I reckon a spell in the Army would do you good··· Make a man o' you it would···'

'Thanks' I say. I pull a face an' for some reason I can't help thinking of that snake with it's guts 'angin' out. I watch the lads outside working together like a little platoon. Join the Army, see the world - an' get bloody shot at. Brilliant. //

6

Foxearth 1982

I say there is no village like it.
Held together by trees, the quiet road
winding its way from Sudbury.
The soft bark of the high wellingtonia
sweet-talking its caress.
The ginger cats blinking, orange-eyed,
at an unexpected car.

In the sun-filled cavity of the
bus shelter, where a Chambers Coach
arrives each Thursday and Friday,
I trace the smooth red brick, the cold flint.
And hearing the solicitor's daughters whooping
in their swimming pool of money,
Mrs Hargreaves hands me the rip
to tear the grass from Harry's grave.

So, treading the tight avenue of limes,
pushing aside the sticky heart-shaped leaves,
I discover this space that now becomes 'head space' -
this little field of death -
shallow undulations pitting the grass,
a broad expanse of primroses
softening the scratched inscriptions. //

Foxearth Churchyard 2011

There is peace,
as though the Twentieth Century has not happened.
The lime trees have sprung to negate it,
to send it away.

There is peace,
even though the sculptured yew trees
speak of Victorian death obsession.
Un-blameworthy if you read the inscriptions:
Consumption, small pox, the death of infants.

This is the barrier set with black drapes,
the hope of trees.

It is John Foster's stage set,
former Victorian pastor
restructuring,
his church re-medievalised with angels,
crowned, my father said, with a High Mass.

But all this blows a pipe dream
just like all the rest.
It is only a repository of human dust.
But beautiful. ⁄⁄

Sarah's Wedding

'Mum!' I says. 'I'm thirteen years old - you can't treat me like I'm some poxy little kid. If I said I didn't wanna come - it's because I didn't wanna come. I said it 'cause I meant it! I didn't want to bloody come!'

'Shut up an' behave' she says, an' before I know it, she shoves this green book in me 'and. 'If you want to a make a noise' she says. 'You can join in the 'ymn just like everyone else…'

'Yer what?' I says. She looks up the front - at the vicar in 'is frock an' the poofter choir boys in their bloody dresses.

'Show some respect for our Sarah…' she says. 'Keep yer big gob shut an' sing…' I give er a look. Well that'll be bloody difficult, won't it? Then some friggin' awful noise breaks out.

'What the 'ell's that?' I says.

'It's the organ' she says. 'Don't you know nothing'? She pokes the book. 'Bloody well sing!' she says, an' everyone starts groaning like they're in pain. I lean towards her.

'Anyway' I says. 'You're right out of order, you are. "Our Sarah"? Since when was she 'our bloody Sarah?' She might be yours - but she sure as 'ell ain't mine. I don't even know 'er. She's the sister of the twenty-fifth boyfriend you've 'ad this year!'

'Chantelle!' she says. 'Stop it! Someone'll hear…'

'You mean Barry'll hear…'

'Quiet!' she says.

'Doesn't 'e know it then?' I whisper. 'Doesn't 'e know he's jus' one of a long line you've been shacked up with this year?' She pulls an ugly face.

'Chantelle!' She whispers it kinda fierce. 'Just behave yourself. We're 'ere now. You, me an' Barry. It's Sarah's wedding an' we're going to bloody well enjoy it whether you like it or not!' I go quiet for a minute. 'Anyway' she says, lookin' a bit 'urt like. 'It's not twenty-five fellas this year - you know very well it's not. It's four - so just you get your facts right!'

'Oh well done, mother' I says. 'That adds up to less than one a month··· Congratulations!' I try an' think back. It's 'ard to remember some o' them. There were Derrick. 'E were a right creep 'e were. She picked 'im up off the internet - drew 'im in wi' that picture she 'ad took ten year ago. Bet the poor bugger 'ad a shock when 'e saw 'er for real! - no wonder 'e disappeared wi' that black woman. An' then there were Dave. 'E were all right. He tried it on wi' me once but I never let 'im. 'How long you been goin' out wi' Barry now?' I whispers.

'Six weeks' she says, an' then she smiles up at 'im like some stupid schoolgirl. Bloody 'ell. Young love, I think to myself. I look at Barry out the corner of me eye.

'How old is 'e?' I says.

'Shush' she says. 'He's forty-three. Now will you pay attention to the bride an' stop asking questions.' Forty-three. I feel a bit queasy in me stomach but I don't say owt.

'Does e know e's younger than you?' I says.

'Shut up' she says. 'Think about the bride··· In't she lovely? Jus' look at 'er' she says. I look at Sarah up there puffed up in white - the way she keeps looking round at people an' grinning.

'The bridegroom's all right' I says. 'An' she'll do I s'pose if you 'appen to like orange foundation. As for that white dress - it's a bit tight across 'er fat arse, don't you think?'

'Shut up. Don't be so rude' she says.

10

'An' thinking about it she can hardly be no spring chicken neither - I mean if Barry's forty-three 'ow old is she?'

'Don't be horrible' she says. 'She's thirty-nine. She's just left it a bit late in life that's all - but every girl deserves 'er day in white' she says. I give 'er a look.

'Bit late? I'd call it a lot late. An' another thing - where'd she get all them bridesmaids?'

'They're 'er *kids*' she says. 'Barry's nieces. You know, from her first two - well not marriages - partnerships.' The 'orrid noise comes to an end an' the vicar starts waffling, giving blessings an' stuff an' reading from a great big book.

'Wearing a white dress is supposed to mean you're a virgin, isn't it?' I says. 'I learnt that in RE - I think it were RE. She's pushin' it in't she, all them kids trailin' after her? Gives the game away on the virgin front, don't you think? Even vicars ain't that daft surely?' Mum doesn't answer, just looks a bit cross like an' ignores me. I think back to them old photos she's got stuffed in a drawer. Pictures of 'er an' dad. I s'pose when she married 'im she kidded 'im she were a virgin. I wonder if 'e believed it? I mean she must've been twenty-seven at the very least, so it wasn't exactly likely was it?

'I s'pose it's only symbolic these days for any woman' I says, tryin' to sound understanding an' worldly-wise like. 'You know - white dresses an' stuff like that.' She gives me a queer look.

'What do you mean?' she says. 'What're you tryin' to say?'

'Well, who the 'ell could wear a white dress these days if it 'ad to be for real? I mean - even I'd struggle wi' that···' Oh bloody 'ell. What've I said? I try an' laugh but she gives me such a look it freezes me. What the 'ell made me say that? I look at her guilty like and 'er eyes drill into mine. Suddenly she ain't whispering no more.

'You little slut' she yells. 'You little bitch! Who the hell was it?' The vicar stops talkin' an' everyone in the church starts lookin'. Talk about embarrassing.

'Mum! Shut up!' I says. She thumps me an' I fall down sideways in the aisle - Barry standin' there lookin' helpless as I sprawl across the carpet.

'Who was it?' she screams, leanin' down an' pullin' me hair. 'Who was the effin' bastard? Tell me!' she yells. Well, I can't *tell* 'er can I?

'No one!' I says.

'Don't effin' lie to your mother!' she shouts. People start dashing about - the bride an' groom comin' down the aisle - the vicar jus' behind. 'Who was it?' she yells. Well, I keep lookin' at Barry but 'e don't move a muscle do 'e? There she is roarin' like a lunatic an' cloutin' me on the head. But suddenly the bridegroom's right beside me - getting himself in between me an' me mum - sittin' me up - an' I can't 'elp but notice 'e smells kinda nice an' even close up 'e's right fit. I look up into 'is deep blue eyes. You don't wanna waste yoursel' on that fat Sarah I think to myself. I mean if she can lie - why can't I?

'It were im!' I shout to the whole church. ''E did it, mum! It were 'im!' 'Is mouth drops open and the whole place goes dead quiet an' I drop smiling deep down into 'is arms··· Well, that were the theory. In fact 'e dropped me an' I banged me 'ead on bloody pew. //

12

Picture This

Tonight she shall be called Euphemia. And he shall be that Dark Knight who never once lifts his visor. How their lives have evolved into this tangle - like a knot of snakes. So many heads and so many tales. How funny they do not realise how mixed up they are.

But Euphemia and her Dark Knight have spread out their gauze. They have turned everything to a species of theatre. How clever their tricks of the light. Each statement just that fateful microbe away from the truth. Falsity so carefully stitched around with mundane veritable facts.

There's a name for this situation. A word deriving from the Old French 'to do'. An affair. And are they doing it? You bet they are.

It's dark. Belief is strange. They enter into the darkness to find their light. Euphemia and he of the visor are like those saintly ones who believe that beyond this death there is another more glorious life. A victory that can be pulled from of the big bag of defeat. But no one ever slits their throat to get there, do they? No. These two dig their tunnels and track their coded passages and carefully preserve the outward show of their lives. For escapees must consider who might save them if the diggings fall. It might have been done a million times, but it's still an unproven scientific process - a tunnel not yet broken through. They do not quite know where they are heading. And so, to them, the slightest whiff of burning boats behind them becomes an acrid and intolerable stench. Some day they may have to come back. Those relationships of old might well be tinder dry, but these two will not yet set the match. Instead they administer this shimmering delusion. This suspension of disbelief.

It is dark, yet strangely in this world of quickly deleted images, they crave something real - to leave some little proof for themselves that this actually did happen. They do not want to say 'this is a lie'. That it never happened. No. Love has triumphed, they have to say - and, let's be honest, love does not triumph just anywhere. Against all odds they have taken this risk - and they have taken it for love. And that little word justifies just about everything, the smoke and the mirrors, the lies and those deliberate confusions.

It is dark. They have brought - a camera. The one thing in this world that never lies. Yes. But at the camera's heart there lies a negative image. That backwards picture of the world. The idea that light is false and black is true.

It is dark. They have put up the gauze and the stage lights mislead the eye. And they have established this little gap behind the wainscot - this area of cold pragmatism - this little cranny of a meeting place. What genii they've become for those spaces behind and between things. Like artists who must draw the gaps and not the things themselves. Making use of useful facts, like the fact that husbands often come home later than their wives. That's called communication time. Then there's the creation of false tradition, like such and such a meeting always taking so long when in fact it's always over in an hour. Or maybe neither of them go at all and they spend a whole three hours together. What luxury! Each must be ready for the word. To snatch the moment. A sleight of hand movement while the audience looks elsewhere. A text on that old pay-as-you-go thing that no one remembers you ever had. Keep it on silent and say nothing. Only consider that awkward but necessary lie that gets you off the spinning plate of the old world. And then the difficulty later in the evening, or next morning, perhaps, of smoothly re-alighting - if that's not too tricky a word.

It's dark. And on this occasion they have brought a camera. And they imprint their negative image on this unseen retina that no one will ever see and they try their best to make something positive out of it. How funny and bleached they look. How the flash obliterates their features - makes them look bug-eyed - and they leap out of their own darkness like neon ghosts. How they laugh. What joy there is in this lie-free zone - what shot of relief bought at so high a price by those hemmed in by their own deceit. Put the camera down, he says, and let's get down to business Missy. Yeah, she says.

The night is black. And the wind is calm on this summer night in this little gap between leaving the pub early from that slightly fictitious 'works do' and the official announcement of having accidentally left it a little late. She and he, colourless and calm. The crunch of stubble as they walk the field where the wind whispers softly in the darkness. Now light is false, black is true. This feeling brings her peace - it unbuttons her soul and she warms her hands on his chest. Together, they cross the bridge, the field, the bridge and they no longer hear the whispering of the grassland, voices like the endless hissing of snakes. Lies, lies, lies. But there is this light here in this darkness. It's so easy to believe in a marital afterlife here where white is black and black is white and the wind is still and Euphemia and her Dark Knight are colourless and calm.

How quickly the brief seconds march along - he hardly has time for his flash. And they promise each other, or simply wish, for other times, longer times, bigger lies. He takes another shot with that camera - she looking dishevelled and rather pleased with herself before the seconds die, and they must leave. Time's oblivion race run begun by the flash of that gun. A camera whose night setting is not all it should be. Pictures of their startled shades shall remain hidden forever on anonymous-looking SD cards forever and forever. One more slim impoverished lie will fold them neatly back into their own beds - into the patina of their outward separation. One clever shake of the solution that shall dissolve them completely, like a magic trick where no watcher can ever really know exactly what he sees. //

Snake

(Girl in Red Approaching)

Snake,
slithering in grassy dimensions.

The girl in red approaching
from some other angle,
some other Marxist glow.

Orange stripe, common snake -
an accusatory glance and grin.

Yes, she and she,
slithering into path,
and out of path.

Some other angle,
some clever intertwining
of tree-ness and knowledge-ness.

At dawn in silhouette.
hanging snake in knowing tree;
waiting for Eve.

Yes, here she comes,
the girl in red
with her wisp of evening.

Her knife always ready
to skin the apple of truth. //

She

(who represents all things irretrievable)

I would often meet her, here at the gate.
in this too-perfect place;
me, bored, and she too I imagine,
tucked away, sitting astride the lych-gate;
she only a girl; me, hardly older,
playing at wisdom.

Talking as twilight fell,
the trees crowding, and dappled shades
inclining - concentrating perhaps
on our gossip, our stilled union;
dusk thickening until we were two
disembodied in a darkness.

But this was not love -
or if it was it was un-stated;
only the clock jagged its quarter hours,
and she, delay after delay,
eventually bowed to night, crept away,
flitted down the avenue of limes.

I do not see her go; hear only her tap-tatting step,
the clack of the far gate;
and though thirty years pass,
I remember how I would strike-up, draw fire;
that pinpoint of a cigarette
the only actual torch I held for her. ⁄⁄

17

Swim

"A man in track-suit appears.
Holds the key
to a vending machine.
A wet-haired crowd
catalogue their losses."

As a non-swimmer, Eric is right out of his depth, bobbing about here in the swimming pool.   Not that he's in the water, you understand. He's in a sort of cafe by the pool and the people 'e's come with 'ave gone for their regular 'works-do' communal splash.   Eric sits 'ere and stirs his coffee - cheap stuff what's so frothy there's no telling what it is.

'Something extracted from the filter system, perhaps?' he thinks, and he looks back to the vending machine where it come from.   It'd made a weird noise when the coins had dropped.   He sighs.   'What am I doing here anyway?' he thinks.   'I mean why come 'ere to this swimming pool when I can't even swim?'

But the answer is simple.   He's here because Sandra - that's Sandra who's married to Simon - Sandra - five foot ten with a pair of knockers fit to die for - Sandra - she says that this little jaunt - this 'works do' will provide the ideal cover.

'Surely that lot'd be better left in the dark?' Eric had said.   'It's no business of theirs, is it?'   But Sandra had got her way.

'Well, if they didn't know before they certainly will now' he says under 'is breath.

He sniffs.   The air's horrible - it's just as bad as this coffee - all frothed-up and scummy somehow - full of chemicals.   'I'd have pushed that

button what said 'de-chlorinated coffee' if that machine had had one'
he says.

Slowly 'is attention wanders. Someone out there's making a right din.
He can hear a swimming instructor's yell bouncing off the rafters. But
he can't hear no words - they're all drowned by the plunging noises -
the hiss and splatter of the water. Eric's disgusted: 'To think people
come to places like this for enjoyment!' He looks about him and his
thoughts drift back to school.

'Come on lad, pull your socks up' he seems to hear Mr Woodhead the
PE teacher saying. ('Snothead' the boys used to call him). 'Listen to
me lad: I've met malingerers like you before···' 'Wanker' thinks Eric.

'But don't you understand?' Sandra had said. 'If it's a works do there'll
be no trouble, will there? I'm just out with 'work', aren't I? And, if we
'appen to get home late - well, all of us, we just stopped off at the pub
on the way 'ome, didn't we? And' she'd added 'I'll have to give you a
lift, won't I?' She'd sort of prodded each word as she said it.

Eric smiles - picks up his coffee - comes back to life a bit. 'Well' he
thinks. 'What's a bit of chlorine between friends when there's the
promise of getting Sandra all to yerself on the back seat of 'er car? I'd
go through some 'igh water for that - sure I would···' His eyes glaze
a bit. A sort of sexual feeding frenzy? - parked up somewhere in the
dark?

Did such moments make it all worthwhile? He don't think about
Sandra's husband - they've not even met - and he certainly don't think
how connected they might be··· Well, Sandra says she don't have sex
at home - but - well, he don't really know, does he?

Suddenly Melissa turns up - 'emerges from the typing pool' Eric jokes
to himself. She plonks herself down, rosy and wet-haired.

'God, that's exhilarating' she says.

'Is it?' says Eric.

One by one 'is workmates come back - all of them - but not Sandra - and they chatter like crazy, nit-picking this thing an' that thing from work an' all looking so bloody 'ealthy and tousled and··· dreary really··· 'Frickin' 'ell' he thinks. 'Where's Sandra?' he asks himself, looking round. But he can't say it out loud. He sits in silence while the rest of them witter. He can't 'take possession' of her like that - not publicly. After all, 'e's only come for the ride.

At last Melissa poses the question for him.

'Where's Sandra?' she says to Marianne and a slight flutter of embarrassment seems to ripple through them - a pebble of doubt sort of plops into their pool. Marianne gives Eric a look, but he keeps a straight face an' she begins to doubt she's got the story between them right.

'I fink she was just talking to that instructor, fellow···' she says, and again, just a little nod, a mere flick of the eye, towards Eric.

But suddenly something else bursts in - it makes Eric laugh - it's a lover's tiff from the next table.

'Where you going?' a blonde girl demands, in a quavery voice. But her boyfriend's whipped off down the stairs an' 'e shows no sign whatever of coming back.

'Where you going?' she wails again. Eric grins.

'That's a laugh' he says to Melissa. But his thoughts filter back. 'Would Sandra really go off with a sort-of PE teacher? A sort of young version of Snothead? Surely not?' He looks at the girl again - an' 'is grief seems to flow and make hers more real to him. He watches - how she looks at her cup - the disgusted way she pushes it across the table. 'Where's Sandra?' he wonders again.

But now there's another sound: A boy who crashes his fists into that vending machine over there. Everyone looks round.

'What the 'ell's up with him?' laughs Eric. But Melissa wants to reassure him.

'She'll be along soon' she says.

'What?' says Eric.

'Sandra!' she says. Marianne intervenes.

'Prob'ly just a passing fancy' she says. 'Don't worry love.' She pats him on the back of his hand. Eric don't answer. It occurs to him that Marianne and Melissa have known Sandra a whole lot longer than 'e 'as. A cloud passes. But a tall man who obviously works 'ere walks across the canteen - he's got a bright blue Nike track suit on and a whistle round his neck.

'Not another frigging PE teacher?' mutters Eric. The man lays a calm hand on the thumping boy and he stops thumping and a load of complainants seem to rise from the tables like a shoal of fish. Suddenly this whole situation begins to make perfect sense.

'There *was* something bloody wrong with that coffee!' Eric says, out loud.

'What?' says Melissa.

'Things never do what they say on the tin, do they?' he complains. Marianne gives him a look. 'That machine's been churning out crap all day - it's been taking everyone's money an' giving cups of shite back in return!' The two girls look confused. It's happened before - this thing with Sandra. Better get used to it, they seem to say. The tall man pours oil on the situation.

'Yes, yes, yes···', he says. He waves a key - opens up the machine and the wet-haired crowd gather to catalogue their losses. Eric looks at Melissa. A little twinkle brightens his eye.

'*She's* all right' he thinks to himself. 'I wonder what *she* might be doing tonight?' ⁄⁄

Age

A Daughter's Visit

Look at us, sitting around the edge of this room. Like wallflowers at a dance, aren't we? We had husbands once, you know. But they've gone - all popped off like your father.

You know, I sit here thinking sometimes. How passive we are! - we don't demand very much, do we? Of course, you'd think we wailed all day if you believed the staff. I suppose we irritate them. They seem to think we're not quite human. Mind you, looking at that old woman there with the teeth hanging out, one can't be surprised⋯ But on the whole we sit here quietly - don't we? - holding on to our little treasures - all those fabulous memories - Suez in the days before the crisis - Singapore with Lionel. Of course, I don't trouble the staff with things like that. Mostly they don't seem interested. After all - they weren't there, were they? - what do they know about things like 'War' and 'Empire⋯?'

The trouble is, you see, they don't listen.

Do you know, by the time I was thirty-three I'd lived through two world wars. Have I told you that before? Yes, in my day, you couldn't just throw money about - you had to 'mend-and-make-do' or jolly well do without! There wasn't all this choice. I told that to the girl who came this morning (you know - the grumpy one) and she looked at me as if I was the daft one!

'Have you seen these?' she said.

'Seen what?' I said - and suddenly I realise she's spinning a pair of pants in the air on the end of her finger! Extraordinary behaviour!

'The whole world will see them if you keep wafting them about like that' I said. She wasn't amused.

'Get your daughter to buy some more.' she said 'They're all holey.'

You know, in my naughty way, I sometimes think we should scream more. That woman over there··· (Well, I was going to say the one with the white hair, but that's rather stupid of me because of course we've all got white hair.) Anyway, that one with the pink cardigan - she screams the place down. Sometimes, you know. It's rather funny. I don't know what's wrong with her. She yells when they take her into tea. And when they take her for a bath, she yells again. She kicked that grumpy carer last week, you know. 'Good for you' I thought. I shouldn't mind kicking her myself. Little minx.

Oh, heavens - look at that - it's that girl with the acne. I've told you about her haven't I! How I wish I could say 'no' when she flops down beside me - flops down like a particularly unruly puppy dog and says: 'Bath time!' Is it really, I say. But it's funny how often I seem to find myself stuck in that poky room with her. I suppose it's because I say 'yes' - but I don't mean to. It's so vexing, isn't it, when you're not in full command of events?

We had that steak pie for dinner again, you know. I've told you about that before, haven't I? It loosens the grip on my upper set. Someone told me, you know - one of the staff I suppose - it comes from a big packet of frozen stuff that simply says 'cubed meat'. What on earth can one make of that? I shouldn't be at all surprised if it were horse or something.

What's that dear? Did I want to complain? Heavens! What for? Oh no, no. You mustn't worry. Everything's fine. They couldn't be kinder. Well, there's nothing to get het up about, dear. They do their best···

You're going to Marks and Spencers to get some pants? What on earth for, dear? For *me*? Yes, yes, I know she said I needed new ones. Yes dear. But it's hardly the place to be talking about pants, is it - in the middle of the lounge! Yes! I do understand what you're saying dear! Well, if you must know, I got my sewing basket out, and I mended them. Well it's my own business, if it's all the same to you,

24

and you seem to forget, madam, that I knew you when you were in nappies! Yes well, we'll just let them drop then, shall we?

What on earth is the matter with you now? I haven't heard anything particularly funny⋯ I mean, are you going to snigger like that for long? Really, you might be my own daughter, but if you've nothing sensible to say, you might just as well not come.

Ah, look who's here - it's that poor girl with the acne - such a distressing condition for a young girl, don't you think? Oh look at her - she's so full of energy isn't she! Like a great big puppy! And really, underneath it all, you know, she's such a sweetie.

What was that she said? Oh, yes, dear, yes. Yes! I'm always ready for a bath! What? My daughter? Oh, don't worry about her - she was just leaving⋯ weren't you dear⋯? ⁄⁄

Pinkness

I sit encased in plush comfort.
The stiff upholstery remains unmoved,-
hardly acknowledging the pressure I exert.
The brand-new carpet glows a ruby red,
weeps a bloody fluff where the wheelchairs run, -
and you flit past in your lilac uniform, -
big and pink, and sweet as seaside rock.

I imagine your care will be diligent,-
nothing will go un-evaluated -
each fragment will be carefully weighed.
Slowly, from these poor remains,
treasuring each fleck of memory,
you will piece together the person I was -
that you will meet me as a friend.

But no - you dart in with your 'Care plans'
'Fluid charts' 'Waterlow scores' and
wrench me from my bed like a tomb robber -
'Time to get up' you say, pulling at the sheets.
Efficiently you wash me here and there,
check for pinkness under breast and groin -
slightly kind, very sweet, effortlessly impersonal.

And swiftly you return me
to this same stiff upholstered chair
which remains as unimpressed as ever.
I feel bewildered, left alone with the bloody fluff
and realising you have so little time.
A quick dust of sweetness is all you can give -
a whiff of seaside rock as you rush away. ⁄⁄

Cloudy Morning before Breakfast

(for Margaret, who packed up everything she owned, every evening...)

Once again you are ready for departure.
The wardrobe empty, and clothes stuffed
in a bursting suitcase. But you haven't
left. Still you linger at this muddy shore -
the watery sky, the grey sea - a slush of
days that bring neither pleasure nor pain.
You look at me doubtfully. Faded eyes
cannot fix the connection we have. The
intervening night has undone it. This is
not your room. Neither these curtains
nor the potted cactus, nor those knots
in the stripped pine. You deny it all.
Slowly I unpack. Cheat, by turning over
objects you've told me about before. 'You
wore this when Alfred got his MBE.' 'Why,
yes' you say 'I believe I did. Fancy you
knowing that.' 'And these shells from the
beach where Bert dropped the ice-cream.'
'Yes!' you say, and an inner sunshine
lights the long drowned day. Carefully we
reclaim the fragments, sift the years. Now
you know when you were born; what
happened to Arthur during the war; that
we can cook eggs here just the way you
like them: 'Sunny side up!' I say. You
beam. 'Come along then' you reply. 'What
are we waiting for?' We laugh and holding
hands, make it to the bedroom door. But

confusion snaps, and still unable to quite
place me, you give me a worried look.
'I say - I haven't *married* you, have I?' ⁄⁄

Day Out of a Lifetime
It Happened in Knaresborough

'What on earth made you choose a great box like that?' says Beryl.

'It was the only one I could find' says Jimmy.

'You sure he's alright in there?'

'Snug as a bug' says Jimmy.

The 36 from Leeds pulls into Harrogate Bus Station and Jimmy gets down, carefully holding the buff-coloured box with a handle he's made out of string. His sister follows.

'Where to now?' she says. 'Another clapped-out bus, I suppose!'

'I've told you before' Jimmy carefully explains. 'Now we're both over sixty, it's best and cheapest way. We might as well get *something* for being old!'

The 101 to Knaresborough waits at the stand. The edge of the box digging into Beryl's ribs as Jimmy takes his seat.

'Watch what you're doing' she complains. Jimmy looks about him.

'There's nothing clapped-out about this' he says. 'Look at the lovely colours⋯ And for that matter there's nothing clapped-out about a 36 either...'

But Beryl isn't listening. She's watching an old lady getting on the bus - an old lady who leans heavily on a pompous-looking man, who seems to be with her, yet somehow has the aura of someone wishing he wasn't. Mother and son, thinks Beryl.

'Here Geoffrey' the old lady says, pointing to a seat. 'Sit here where we won't get jogged. We don't want Hercules getting sick, now do we?'

'Perish the thought, mother' says Geoffrey, dismissively. They sit down in the seats beside Jimmy and Beryl, the old lady mostly hidden by a similar box that Geoffrey keeps balanced on his knee, just as Jimmy does.

'Well, look at that!' says the old lady. 'That gentleman's got a box just like ours - isn't that extraordinary?'

'Fascinating…' says Geoffrey, not bothering to look.

'It's not fair to leave them at home is it? I always take Hercules with me' she says. Jimmy and Beryl smile across the aisle. The bus sets off.

'You've got a pussy cat in there, haven't you?' the old lady says, and she taps on her own box and pokes her finger through a hole. 'You don't like being stuck in this nasty old box, do you… No!' Hercules begins to caterwaul.

'Quiet, mother' says Geoffrey, crossly. 'Leave the thing alone.'

'What sort is yours?' the old lady asks.

'Oh, just an ordinary sort' Beryl replies.

'A grey one' says Jimmy.

'Oh, is it a Persian?' Beryl looks at Jimmy, then down at the box.

'You're alright, aren't you dear?' she says to the cardboard. But the box says nothing. Meanwhile Hercules has broken into a pitiful wail.

'I told you not to disturb it' says Geoffrey. He gives the box a sharp smack with the flat of his hand and the wailing stops immediately. His mother looks at him, daggers.

'Your's is very quiet' she says to Jimmy.

'Oh yes. He's very sleepy nowadays' says Jimmy. 'But then, none of us are getting any younger…'

'Good Lord, no - I'm ninety next birthday' she says with pride. 'And Hercules will only be five - won't you my little darling?' Once again she scratches at the box and Geoffrey irritably pulls it away from her.

'Is Uncle Geoffrey being nasty? He's a naughty boy isn't he!' Then, suddenly, she drops her voice. 'He's just like his father, you know!' she says. 'Geoffrey's father left us in the lurch! Oh yes! Geoffrey was only a little boy - weren't you Geoffrey?'

'Mother! Please! I'm sure the whole bus doesn't need to know that.' But actually the whole bus is fascinated.

'Boys *will* always end up like their fathers, won't they?' she says.

The bus goes on and the old lady's monologue lapses. Geoffrey looks neither left nor right, as if a brick wall separates one side of the bus from the other, his face as unsmiling as any face could be. But suddenly, as they reach Bond End his mother is off again. She bursts into a speech as if she's on stage.

"Agnes! That's it, Agnes!' he shouted. *'I've had enough - I'm leaving!'* And so he did - right then and there - right out of the blue! And poor Geoffrey here - still in short trousers!'

'Mother!' says Geoffrey. Jimmy whispers to Beryl from the side of his mouth.

'Agnes and Geoffrey indeed! What a couple! Miserable fellow! If I'd been his father I'd have done the same…' Beryl nudges him in the ribs and looks out of the window, trying not to laugh.

The crowded bus stops outside Sainsbury's and the two men with their big boxes move sidelong down the aisle. Beryl helps the old lady down.

'We haven't heard much from you, have we?' she says, tapping the lid of Jimmy's box. 'I do hope he's alright. Next time you should put some holes in it!'

'Yes' says Jimmy. 'Thank you. I'll bear it in mind.'

31

What a relief it is to be in Knaresborough at last, and left to their own devices.

'That Geoffrey seemed a right old grump, didn't he?' says Beryl.

'Aye' says Jimmy. 'Now where's this castle we're looking for?'

They cross over into Silver Street and walk along.

'There's a sign down there' says Beryl, pointing towards the library.

They move on and the trail takes them past the Police Station into a square full of parked cars.

'There it is!' says Jimmy, looking up. 'There's our castle.' But instead of picking up their steps, a sudden gloom seems to descend. They look at each other. Setting out on this journey was one thing. Arriving is something else.

'Let's sit on a bench' says Beryl, and Jimmy waits patiently as she composes herself. They look about them, uncomfortably. It's a strange, solemn moment.

'Right' she says, opening her handbag, and taking a deep breath. She pulls out an envelope and reads aloud what it says on the front.

"The final wishes of Herbert Arthur Roebottom, to be read at Knaresborough Castle, North Yorkshire, after my decease." Again she hesitates. Eventually she opens the seal. Jimmy clutching the box ever more tightly.

'My dear children' Beryl reads. *'I hope you will always feel that you were loved by your old father, and I hope you will always love him in return, however little you may now think he deserves it.'* Beryl looks up apprehensively to find Jimmy looking back, transfixed. She reads on.

"The truth is I was not a good man, and I am sorry I have been too cowardly to tell you this like a man, and have resorted to writing you this dreadful letter. During the War, I was stationed near

32

Knaresborough where I met and married a lovely lady, a couple of years before I met your own dear mother. Put it down to weakness if you like but I wanted them both and couldn't choose. Only after five years did I leave the first woman to be with you and your mother, full time. I have a son - your half brother. I want you to find him and give him all the money I have left. I know this is hard on you, but you had the benefit of my presence all your days whereas he did not. It's the guilt you see, and perhaps I can recompense him a little from beyond the grave. I hope you will do this and not hate me. Your dear father, Herbert Arthur Roebottom.''

Beryl lets the paper drop. She gazes across the putting green. A little spot of crimson grows in the centre of each cheek.

'The old *bastard!* she declares. Suddenly some nervous energy seems to flash through her. Jimmy sits, still clutching the box, looking stunned but infuriatingly docile.

'Hand over all our money to strangers we don't even know?' she shouts. 'Is that what he means us to do? Does he really expect us to go looking for this son of his? The man's mad!'

'The man's dead' says Jimmy.

'It's ridiculous!'

'We don't have any choice' says Jimmy.

'Don't have any choice? I'll show you what choice we've got! The 'benefit of his presence' indeed!' Suddenly, before Jimmy can react, Beryl stands up and snatches the precious box from his grip. With amazing strength she rips it open and flings the entire contents at the nearest waste paper bin. A plume of white dust flies up like smoke.

'Hey!' says Jimmy. 'He didn't say to scatter his ashes in the waste bin! Look here - there's a P.S. - we're supposed to scatter them in the shrubbery - it's where he used to meet Agnes, during the war! It says here!'

'*Agnes?*' says Beryl. Her anger collapses. Suddenly brother and sister go absolutely pale. They stare at each other in shocked silence.

'Not Agnes⋯' says Jimmy.

'Not Hercules⋯' says Beryl. Then in a moment of utter despair they reach the same dread thought.

'And not *Geoffrey!!*' they cry in unison. For a moment they're frozen. They stare in horror. But Jimmy quickly comes to his senses. He pulls out his cigarette lighter. Urgency returns.

'Here, quick, give me the letter' he says. 'No one else knows a word of this. Let's get shot of it. Come on, Beryl, kick the ash around - pick up the casket.' She does as she's told. The letter flames. 'Let's get out of here. Let's get the bus' he says.

'Bus?' she replies. 'You must be joking⋯ If I ever catch another bus in Knaresborough it'll be a day too soon.' She pulls out a roll of banknotes she's kept with the offending letter. 'We'll go by *taxi*' she says. 'And Herbert Arthur Roebottom can bloody well pay for it!' //

Floodlight: Vic Reeves' Wonderland:

Singing Strawberry Fair.
(Illuminating York 2012, The Museum Gardens)

The big screen of the Yorkshire Museum.
Singing, singing, buttercups and daisies.
The constant refrain, and the rain
like little bulbs of squirted light
precipitating into this wonderland
the paths so bright with lamps
singing, singing, buttercups and daisies.

Only a month or so ago
this would've been truly sub-aqua
this bright-lit low path by the river
flooded with murk and danger
brimful of such a muddy dark.
Now it is filled with light and
singing and buttercups and daisies.

But, Vic, what exactly is this song?
as your words explode into fractures
and the splintered crowd wander
(singing, singing), from one sea
of light refreshments to the next?

Is this some citadel? - Eboracum en-fete?
Pushing out the darkness of uncertainty?
Yes! We will project it away! -
capture ourselves dancing,
cascading into this shower of pixelated light,
split particles of some great whole.
Yes. Together we are lightness itself. ⁄⁄

Locomotion

(Illuminating York 2012, National Railway Museum)

What roaring is this
in this darkness?
This evocation of half-lit,
half-forgotten stations,
of missed connections
and lost journeys?

Alas, it is not real.
None of these old locos
have fire in their belly.
All movement is illusion.
They are back-lit, front-lit,
carefully preserved.

But how they refuel
the thrill of the night train
roaring past - flashing -
(and flashed at
by these enthusiasts cameras),
they find their spark.

Yes, listen. Tonight
the beasts are restless.
Their fire boxes fume,
they shunt memory,
pound between the lines,
the air thick with an oily smoke.

I would like to think
it is always like this,
when the doors are closed,
and the anorak crowds have gone,
that these cowed beasts
puff out their grandeur. ⁂

A Hill of Ash

Sir Christian has come to the churchyard to open the vault of his ancestors. They are detached from their shadows. How they shout down the white blank spaces of the snow. But to reach their bones a trench must be dug immediately outside the transept wall of the village church.

Old Mr Siddle, his workman, breaks the ground and Sir Christian sees the fecundity of the shifted soil - how it grows shovelful after shovelful. And then the hollow thumping of a crowbar on stone. Like some archaeologist, Mr Siddle breaks through and, shying away from the hot breath of the arc light, Christian sees for the first time how sterile is this little room. How neat. How dank a smell that now rushes to his senses.

The walls are whitewashed, though somewhat discoloured. No one has penetrated this space for full eighty years. And yet metaphorically it's the place where everyone comes. In this odd moment it seems to Christian not just a hole in the ground but some unclimbable mountain.

'We've not had a family entombment here since 1932' he tells his man, in his usual posh, projected voice. Mr Siddle scrapes his shovel.

'I'm surprised it's still dry' he grunts, rather too practically, perhaps.

'Good to get back to the old traditions, though, don't you think⋯?' says Christian. 'My family have had connections with this village for full seven hundred years, you know - though this vault here is only Victorian of course⋯ And I like to think that your great-grandfather did the same service with his shovel for my great-grandfather as you've just done for me. Five generations, you know, your family have worked for mine, Mr Siddle⋯'

The workman says nothing. Breaking open the past like this has made him feel uncomfortable. Or maybe it's this living man that does that. He backs away. Drags his spade away into the sweet light of the churchyard. He sits on a lichen-covered stone to await developments. Thus Sir Christian Critchley-Cleverton, the fourteenth baronet, is left in sole possession of his tomb.

There are eight coffins here - four Critchleys perhaps, and four Clevertons (who knows?), closely packed together, and not room for any more. At some point someone in the family must've known this, for Sir Christian's parents and grandparents have all been buried elsewhere. But Christian himself has not known it. He shrugs. Great Aunt Beatrice will have to wait her eternity on a trolley in the corridor, he surmises, just as she had done for her final fifteen hours at A&E.

'Oh, well. She'll not know a thing about it, will she?' he says out loud.

He's disappointed really - how long has he waited for this moment? From a little boy he's felt fascinated by this room hidden beneath the foundations of the church, pressured by the weight of the Fifteenth Century transept. A special family room where no other Critchleys or Clevertons have ever ventured willingly. It's more cramped than he's expected. Less a shrine - more a storage unit.

But a new disturbance eats away at his composure - and it's not the thought of ghosts. No. Nothing here threatens to leap out at him. In fact quite the contrary. It's the profound inaction that alarms him. In eighty years when the world outside has leapt forward buzzing with life, and the Critchley-Cleverton fortune has dwindled somewhat, nothing - absolutely nothing - has stirred within these walls. A little gritty dust has fallen like a thin layer of snow and that is all.

But Life has a habit of refusing Death the permanence due to it. Life cannot stand the idea that it's extinguished forever. Death must be given a voice. Thus this hole in the ground seems no hole at all. It is a hill. And Sir Christian suddenly sees it as a place where not only his relatives lie, but everyone else's too. They have been carried here one by one. Box after box. It is a hill of ash, a hill of bones, a buzzless beehive of grey hair.

He hears them. Yes. Since he will not have them silent, he hears them - shouting from this tangle. And he sees the utter absurdity of keeping his family bones exclusive from all others.

'No, no, no!' they seem to yell. 'You cannot do this. What are you preserving us for? You cannot look upon us. We will shoot down our shadow selves and forbid you our mountain. You shall not come here with your blood and your pinkness and your cosy thoughts and your family relationships. For all that is now anathema to us. We cannot allow it. We will keep you away with the net of our shadows. We who do not even know who it is we lie with…'

'Look away. You will not rise. You will come here alone. Disconnected, shorn of life. We have kept this place neat and clean for you, and we have not changed anything at all.'

So the dead seem to speak to Sir Christian in his family vault. And they speak it without moving their mouldy lips, in this little room wedged beneath the Fifteenth Century transept.

'I say! I say!' he suddenly calls, unexpectedly needing the live companionship even of his old family retainer. 'I say - Mr Siddle…!'
The old man rises from his grave - looks suspiciously through a veil of haughty subservience at his so-called master - as he emerges from the fresh dug hole.

'Ah, there you are…' says Sir Christian, laughing a self-deprecating laugh. 'You don't believe in ghosts do you, Mr Siddle?' The old man bequeaths him a splendidly dead-pan look.

'Not exactly' he says. 'Mother said 'twere the livin' you 'ad to worry about, sir…'

'Ah!' laughs Sir Christian, uncomfortably. 'Indeed! Yes! Ha ha!' But the amusement dies on his lips.

A Shift in September

The night infests the day this September morning.
Dark that will not leave. Yet alarms yell 'out! out!'
And dragging the smell of soft sheets we pull on
these uniforms. Practical blue trousers that unshape
the loveliest legs. Tunics of sour green. Creep away
from Acomb on buses, half asleep - walk down from
the heights of Badger Hill. Drive in, irritated. Park.

Wake up! Wake up! The shrill buzz of disordered
routine insists we leave all thoughts of home. Here!
care plan! - bowel regimen! - the numbers are not
good - so-and-so is off sick - we must allocate time
sparingly - a thin-stretched layer of care - time will
drum on it till it shreds - over-hung heads must
forget themselves. Come on now - shift - shift!

So I am pounded like a nail into the soft quiet of
your room on this dark September morning. You
lie there blinking as I did once, yet worse for you
with those wounds multiplied in your brain and
needing me, or us, or someone, to help with every
detail. In bed, with nothing save a sweaty shift,
we are alike. Vulnerable. Exposed. Open to attack. ⁄⁄

Cats

A voice from the street jabs.

'Cat's pee!' it shouts, but Marjorie Fleming isn't listening.

'What year is it now?' she's wondering. She's amazed. How can she not know what year it is? She looks down the long avenue of trees. How they've grown! She's been walking along Hookstone Road for ever so long. But for how many years? She can't remember.

'Take a whiff of that! Pure cat's piddle, that is!' calls the voice, but Marjorie Fleming's train of thought won't be deflected.

'The war's over⋯ And eventually Mr Churchill got re-elected, didn't he?' she says to herself. With an immense effort, she recalls it had once been 1955. Something must've happened then, but she can't think what. Now it's later. 1958 perhaps? She would've gone back to buy a newspaper to check, but it's too far, and the knitted bag of heavy cat food is pulling on her arm.

Today, she's been lucky. The grocer has been selling off bashed tins of Kat-i-can. True, one of them seems blown, but a penny in your purse is always better than one in old Mr Sansom's till. A green car whips past and at last she realises someone is shouting.

'Here kitty, kitty!'

Her heart sinks. It's that boy with the red hair. How she wishes she could wipe that smirk clean off his face. She's frightened really, but she knows above all she must keep her dignity. She ignores him - fixes her attention on the distant junction of Hookstone Road and Oatlands Drive and walks on.

'What's that smell of fish?' the boy jeers. 'Oh yes, it's the cat lady!'

Marjorie catches sight of him. Luckily, he's on his own with no one to show off to. She concentrates on her steady course.

43

'Fag ash and cat's pee!' he calls. 'Can you lick your own bum, cat woman?' His voice trails off and Marjorie is relieved. At least that means he isn't following. She hurries on - not at all keen on being out. She loves her little house, even though it's got so dilapidated. Once it had been beautiful.

She goes to the back door and turns the key. The excitement in the house is palpable. Mr Sharp-Ears is up first, with Ginger McCleesh not far behind. Excitement entices other cats into the kitchen. Soon the whole floor is a restless sea of fur - tails pointing up like periscopes.

'Alright, alright - let me in⋯' she says. The cats purr and meow - rubbing their glossy flanks against her legs. There's nothing for it. She'll have to feed them straight away. She sits down on the sofa while the cats leap, giving voice to a yowling serenade.

The tin-opener lies where she's left it - a large spoon beside it on the table. She opens six cans and tips the contents into six dirty bowls which form a semi-circle round her feet. The cats tuck in - some sharing - others getting a bowl to themselves. Then Marjorie opens another, first checking it's not the blown one. She stares intently at the contents, sighs, and raises one of the meaty chunks to her lips.

It isn't bad this Kat-i-can stuff - better than the Fishy-Meal-For-Cats she'd tried once before. That was awful. It had made her sick and Thomas Whitelegs had had to clean the carpet for her. But she doesn't feel much like eating. What she really needs is a fag.

She lights up and surveys the room. It's a mess. She knows it. But nobody important ever comes, so what does it matter? The last time she'd looked in the bathroom there'd been a thick mat of cobwebs over the taps and the bath was brown. A sudden impulse makes her puts the fag down and she slips off a shoe. The foot of her stocking is almost black and underneath it her skin is streaked with dirt. She touches the yellow accumulation on the back of her ankle, takes another drag, spits on her fingers, and smears the tarry saliva into the dead skin. Slowly it comes away, leaving a trail of whitish flecks on the sofa and the carpet. Blackie Ringtail comes to investigate - he sniffs suspiciously and wisely decides to settle at a distance. Ginger McCleesh jumps up on the dining room table and stretches himself out luxuriously. Marjorie lights a second cigarette from the butt end of the first.

Soon it will be time for her visitor. Not a real visitor, of course, just someone she sees.

Gradually she stiffens as she waits. She has the most awful laugh this girl. It's a torment that Marjorie doesn't exactly feel she deserves. What Leonard had seen in the minx she couldn't fathom. Men! Well, maybe they weren't all bad - but Leonard had been - a real stinker. She knows this visitor will come tonight and, as ever, Marjorie will confront the little madam full in the face.

The seconds stretch and Marjorie gets tense, until a jewelled hand runs down the edge of the door at the entrance to the hall. A throaty laugh bubbles up as if Leonard has touched the girl somewhere he shouldn't - a laugh that tells him he's a naughty boy, but he can touch her there any time he likes. Dirty whore, thinks Marjorie. In she bounces - still young in that awful A.T.S. uniform - so sensual, blooming and shiny. Marjorie is sickened. But she's determined never to be upset.

The performance proceeds. Here's the girl, flitting about in her artful way, as empty-headed as ever, dancing a sort of jitterbug. She giggles, but doesn't speak - never quite looks Marjorie in the eye. In turn, Marjorie stares back as resolutely as she can. She watches, until after ten minutes the girl pulls up her khaki skirt - flashes her stocking tops, and disappears back into the hall. Does she jitterbug her way up the stairs for some ritual tumble in the sheets with Leonard? Marjorie no longer cares. They both deserve each other.

The next visitor, however, is more of a problem. Almost as soon as the A.T.S. girl has gone, the swing in the garden begins to creak. It's a gentle sound, and it arises from a point directly behind the sofa - beyond the ragged net curtains and the dirty windows. The child who swings there obviously moves in a leisured and dreamy fashion. Marjorie has no need to see who it is. She knows exactly. Soon the pleading will begin.

'Mummy⋯. Mummy⋯. are you there, Mummy?' It's Oswald. How that voice pierces her soul. She knows he's dead - he died in the war - of course he did⋯ And yet he calls her. What does he want?

'Mummy⋯ Oh, Mummy, where are you? Mummy⋯ '

Marjorie can't look, but she sees Little Oswald swinging there just as he had done a few short years before, when their days had been happy - before they'd both realised how treacherous the world could be. But Leonard's villainy is nothing - let him dance the jitterbug with any floozy he chooses - Marjorie no longer cares. But she feels she's let down this little boy. The tears run down her cheeks - so desperate is she to respond - and yet she can't - because he's dead. He can't possibly be there. It's all happening in her head. She knows that. It's a mad head. It sees things and hears things that aren't there. How can she go on facing the world with a mad head?

Three days later, whilst again sitting stiffly on the sofa awaiting her visitors, Marjorie is distracted by an unusual noise from the kitchen.

'Ginger McCleesh?' she calls out, quietly. 'Is that you?' But Ginger McCleesh is laid on the dining room table as usual. He looks up, slitty-eyed and drunk with sleep. Then there's a loud clatter and all the sleeping cats look up as one. With remarkable agility Marjorie leaps over the back of the sofa and drops into the space behind it. Someone is in the kitchen, and she knows this time it's no apparition, but flesh and blood.

Everything goes quiet. Marjorie can't see from where she's hidden, so she crawls to the far end of the sofa and peers from under the arm rest.

'It stinks of cat's pee!' a voice whispers.

46

'What did you expect? She won't 'ave nothin' anyway···'

'You don't know, there might be wads of fivers in a mattress···'

'It stinks.'

'Shut up will you? Now. Listen. Where is she?'

A head pops stealthily into the room and looks around. Marjorie immediately recognises the red-headed boy from down the road. A chill spreads through her.   What has he come for? She fears what he might do, especially as there are no wads of fivers to be found in a mattress. But she also fears what she might have to do to him - should push come to shove. She keeps low, frightened to breathe.

'There's no one here - only loads of cats' says the boy.

'Crikey! Look at the dirt on this carpet!'

'Looks like someone's been sick on it.'

'I can hardly breathe.'

'Have a look around - she can't just live on fresh air···'

'She certainly don't do that!' says the other boy, waving his hand under his nose. Suddenly he seems to change his mind. 'Look, I'm not touching this - you could get typhoid or cat's flu or something - let's get out···'

'No, no. Think about the mattress - if we only found two fivers it'd be worth it···'

'Let's get away from these cats at least - I don't like the way they're looking at me.'

'Better than dogs. Come on. There must be stairs through here.'

The two boys creep through the hall doorway - followed by the alert saucer eyes of nineteen cats. Marjorie watches too. She knows the red-headed lad, of course, but the other is a stranger - taller with mousey hair - not quite so bold.

'We should've come when she was out - that's what we should've done…'

'Don't worry. We can deal with cat woman if we have to - no problem.' Cautiously, the boys begin to climb the stairs. Marjorie can see their thick socks through the open hall door, their dark heavy boots. Suddenly they jump as Fleecy Thomas shoots down the stairs. Fleecy is new and rather nervous. The animal skids on the accumulated fur at the bottom of the stairs and hides himself amongst the other cats, like a leaf in a tree.

'Flip me! I wondered what that was…' says the taller boy.

'Just another cat…' says the other. He begins to ascend once more - the tall boy carefully keeping three steps behind.

Meanwhile, Marjorie Fleming has crept from her hiding place. She's slipped under the dining table on all fours and woven her way through the dusty tie bars that cross beneath it like an 'x'. She's anxious not to clatter the legs that hold the extra leaves when the table is folded out. Carefully, she reaches the hall door and closes it without a sound. She sits on the floor, her back pressing the door and surveys her legion of cats. The cats look back, waiting. For a moment all is still.

Then, from upstairs, a sudden squeal breaks the tension, and the cats begin to fly wildly round the room. They hiss and spit, clambering over each other in a rush to come together. Quickly, they arrange themselves like a huge fur mantle around the feet of Marjorie Fleming. The two boys clatter down the stairs - something has panicked them - and their panic becomes absolute terror when they realise the door to the lounge is closed and a heavy weight holds it shut.

'The front door' the tall lad shouts. 'Open the front door!' But the read-headed boy is already there pulling at it. But it doesn't budge - it's locked and all the bolts are nailed down.

'It's no good!' says the ginger boy. 'We'll have to get out the same way we came in … And it can only be cat woman - an old woman -

48

that's all···' They both fling themselves at the door. It resists, but eventually, inch by inch, it begins to move until suddenly it gives way altogether and the first lad falls headlong into a sea of cats. Fur is everywhere and his orange hair seems to merge into the orange of the ginger cats. The tall lad trips too, closing his eyes in terror - flinging out his arms. The warm fur wraps him. He knows they will tear into his flesh - rip him to shreds. But they don't. He opens his eyes. He sees the ginger lad transformed - still human but fiery orange. He tries to yell but the noise that comes is merely the shriek of a frightened cat. He feels the bones inside him changing into cat bones.

Marjorie's new cats are always nervous. Whether it's because some part of them remains human, she can't tell, but they soon slip into the ways of cats - thinking only of warm places, of comfort and the hand that feeds. Twenty-two cats, thinks Marjorie. Of course, this can't go on.

The unexpected commotion has kept the A.T.S. girl away, but as Marjorie settles again and the cats lazily close their eyes; the familiar creak of the garden swing brings her back to normality. As ever, it follows the usual pattern. A few moments of gentle swinging and then the one voice Marjorie cares most for in the world.

'Mummy··· Mummy - are you there, Mummy···?' The tears burn her cheeks. She can easily draw in these strangers - knit them neatly into the fabric of her feline family - but the one other human she really desires, remains forever beyond reach.

'Mummy··· Mummy···'

Marjorie looks about the room. The black and white cats are grouped together by the kitchen door. Do they realise they were all once policemen? Scraggy had been an over-pushy Jehovah's Witness. The grey ones had once represented the Borough Council, and the ginger ones··· Well, they were merely scavenging males - insurance men and such-like - now augmented by the red-headed boy from Hookstone

Road. She's rather pleased she's got him at last. What pleasure it will give her to see him lick his own 'bum', as he puts it. Marjorie smiles. Generally she regrets having to add to her furry family - it means struggling home with more tins of Kat-i-can - but now that wretched boy will be eating out of her hand.

Oswald's voice fades away after fifteen minutes, and Marjorie feels guilty that her thoughts have been distracted. She lights a cigarette. She wants to relax but some doubt lingers in her mind. It troubles her. Is it still that question of what year it is? No. It's something else.

The sight of her two most nervous cats, looking uncomfortable in the middle of the room, suddenly brings to mind what it is that worries her. No other intruder has ever got upstairs - usually she deals with them because they've asked awkward questions or annoyed her in some way. Slowly something begins to crystallise in her mind. It is up there⋯ Something upstairs has frightened them. But what? She knows there's some reason why she almost never goes there - but in the press of organising the cats, she's forgotten what it is. Marjorie looks at the dirty ceiling - does her best to penetrate its network of fine cracks. A horrid feeling begins to grow in the pit of her stomach - it's something she's felt before - some while ago - and yet she's damped it down and put it away.

She rises from her seat. The cats sense that something odd is happening. Marjorie Fleming seems to hover above the sofa, seems to glide across the room towards the hall door. Ginger McCleesh's tail spreads like a fan and the hair stiffens along his entire backbone. The other cats rise from their sleeping places one by one, alert and ready. Marjorie Fleming leads the way - something 'up there' draws her. Her feet hardly touch the stairs, only her bony hand etches a faint line through the dust on the banister. The cats follow like a fur mantle spreading spikily behind her - drawing themselves along, brimming with static.

At the top of the stairs, Marjorie lifts her head. She looks at the yellowing doors of her three forgotten bedrooms - cobwebs hang in sheets - and there are boys' footsteps in the thick dust, and one bedroom door stands wide open.

Ah, yes···

Leonard and the A.T.S. girl are still in bed - Marjorie can see them - dusty - but still showing some semblance of substance beneath the sheets. The awful truth spears into her mind. Of course, of course··· It had gone on too many years - the thin A.T.S. girl had grown plump but still Leonard had bedded the fat cow. Marjorie had been sickened - in her own bed too! Twelve years it had gone on - twelve bloody awful years - until 1955.

Of course. It had once been 1955...

Marjorie turns and screams. And the scream tears through the sea of fur - it rips the mantle from her back and the cats scatter. All at once, the red-headed boy is back. The policemen are back. Council officers mill in the hallway. Even the Jehovah's Witness is back. They're all chattering, amazed to find English once more spouting from their mouths. Suddenly ideas of comfort, of milk and Kat-i-can, are displaced by earlier, stranger thoughts. The Council men tut-tut at the dirt, the Jehovah's Witness praises God and the policemen suddenly think of crime scenes, and witnesses, and taking statements.

Marjorie Fleming never hesitates. She runs straight into the garden.

'Mummy! Mummy!' cries Oswald as he slips from the swing. She hugs him, clasps him tightly, for now she will never let him go. Never has she felt so happy - so, so happy - and she doesn't even care that Blackie Ringtail in the guise of a policeman is bearing down on her with such a solemn look. ⁄⁄

Adolescence Again

Skydive

(Youth leaps from the parental aeroplane)

We claim not to have flown at all.
No, our feet never left the ground.
Life, we believe, is thrilling enough
without this unnerving descent.
We would see you float like gossamer.
As gentle yet, as a little seed
blown smooth upon the breath of God.

Instead, you fly like a missile -
like an asteroid with flaming tail.
The air is not nothing as you jump -
it is solid and resents your flight.
You must hack your way through it.
It is the roar of fifty thousand fans -
a hundred jet engines scream in the sky.

Come down then, adrenalin junkie -
fill our hearts with cold horror!
Open up a passage from youth to death -
press that button of self-destruction!
Our thoughts and fears are not quelled
knowing youth must challenge death
and, on landing, grin about it. //

Jim the Joiner

I thought it was fellas what were supposed to get *women* into bother! Chance would be a fine thing, I tell you. You see I'm pushing me trolley down the aisle in Morrisons an' who do I bump into? Amy! (that's me ex-Mrs.) and I've not seen her for six months.

'It's the odd-job-man!' she says.

'Very funny' I says. She calls me that 'cause I do a bit o' this an' that in 'ousehold repairs, you know, - an' that leads up to 'er punch line don't it?: "You certainly made an odd job o' being married to me!" she says. Oh, ho, ho, ho. It takes two to tango, I tell 'er···

'You gonna come an see me in a play?' she says.

'What?' I says.

'I joined the Drama Group!' she says. 'Didn't I tell you? Come an see me make a pranny of myself. Mind you' she says. 'I never got the part I auditioned for. These little groups are always the same, you know. I wanted to be the lead - but Tina flippin' Hogworthy got that - as usual.'

'Tina Hogworthy?' I says. 'Who's she?'

'She's a fat cow!' she says. Amy smiles at me, (in fact, just like she used to). 'You comin' then?' she says. 'It'll only cost you a fiver.'

So two weeks later I'm in this stuffy little hall waitin' for the curtain to go up on somethin' called "Millicent Dissembles" - whatever that is. I look at me programme. Oh··· I see she's gone back to 'er maiden name. Oh, an' 'ere's Tina Hogworthy - playin' the lead part of Millicent it says. The lights go down.

It's kinda weird you know, lookin' at yer ex-Mrs when she can't see you back. Not sure as I would've recognised 'er really. Makes me realise that I never really knew 'er even when we was married. But it's funny, innit, 'ow sometimes you can't quite stop feelin' connected.

But blow me if something don't 'appen what knocks me ex clean out me 'ead. Tina Hogworthy makes 'er entrance, don't she? The famous Tina Hogworthy··· She comes on, an' would you believe it, she's 'ardly got a stitch on - there she is in 'er bra an' knickers - an' she starts doin' this sort of TV workout routine.

'Blimey!' I says out loud.

'Shush···' someone says. Now there's a fine figure of a woman I think to myself. No wonder Amy didn't get the part. This Tina's got sommat, you know. She's one o' them women what's "as it', as they say. Pwoar, I could watch 'er bouncing about all evening. But she covers up, don't she, an' after that I kind of lose interest.

But I phone Amy next morning.

'You was good!' I says. But I kinda get the feeling she's still sore about not getting that part, an' she wants me to say that Tina Hogworthy was crap.

'Rolling 'er flab about the stage like that!' she says. But I don't rise to it. I don't give 'er the satisfaction, so she's a bit off with me. Ooh, I think. Bit sensitive about our Tina are we?

'You got any odd jobs need doing···' I says.

'Look' she says. 'If I 'ad any jobs I'd call someone what was competent to do 'em···'

'Please yourself···' I says.

Back in Morrison's a week or two later, a sort of vision pops up before me. A woman I've kind of seen before.

''Ello Millicent!' I says. Lead artiste Tina Hogworthy 'as to do a quick double take don't she?

'I beg your pardon?' she says.

55

'I loved that play you were in' I says. 'What a performance!' 'Er face lights up.

'Of course!' she says. '"Millicent Dissembles!" You really enjoyed it?'

'I thought you were wonderful' I tell her. She smiles.

'Would you believe it' she says, 'I've been in that drama group for five and a half years and this is the first time I've ever been stopped by a fan! How lovely!' And we gets talking don't we? And by the time we've stood there 'alf an 'our an' she's asked me if I'm handy with the odd *tool*, well, I kinda get the impression she's got the hots for me. I'm gonna be her secret weapon, she says⋯ Can we meet down the rehearsal rooms? Okay I says.

'I'll wait for you outside' she tells me.

We burst in. An' I'm wondering what our Amy's gonna make of this little conquest of mine. There's all these arty types 'angin' about - Amy amongst them - an' Tina makes 'er entrance - (I guess she does that wherever she goes.)

'It's Jim the Joiner!' she shouts, introducing me. 'We're never short of performers are we boys and girls - but set-builders are like gold-dust!'

'Yer what?' I says. But they all crowd round me like I'm royalty, an' I can't help but grin. An' there's Amy - 'er eyes drilling into mine. Ooh, 'ave I pigged you off by any chance?

'Jim the Joiner?' she mouths. 'Jim the friggin' bob-a-jobber, more like⋯' I laugh. What does it matter to me?

'I've pulled your star performer!' I tell 'er. 'I'm moving on - and it's *you* what's gone backwards to your maiden name⋯' But she pulls me to one side.

'For your information' she says, 'Tina Hogworthy is gay.' I give 'er a look. 'She's *gay!*' she repeats. 'Could you not tell, you great pillock! When she says she wants you for your screwdriver that's exactly what she means!'

'What?' I says. 'But··· I thought she meant one o' them double entendre things···'

'You great tosser' she says. 'She wants you to build the sets!'

'Come along, Jim' calls Tina. She's 'olding up this great big bit o' wood. 'I thought we could start' she says, 'by filling in these old screw holes··· Are you good with screw holes?'

'Brilliant' I says, without much enthusiasm. 'Just brilliant···'

An' Amy gives a hollow laugh··· ⁄⁄

Geoff Cousins' Crisis

Geoff Cousins is asleep in bed. The men in uniform are asking questions. It's the threshold of a plane, and a curved door lies half open and two men stand there with clipboards glowing with conceited authority. Geoff Cousins is annoyed. And yet the three of them stagger as the aircraft seems to bank sharply to the right - an aircraft they're not even on.

'Well, how confusing is that?' Geoff thinks to himself. But the obstinate men remain focussed. 'Look, I just don't know the answers' Geoff tells them. 'Is that clear? I don't know!'

What a relief it is to wake up. The plane and the men take off somewhere and Geoff can feel the warmth of the duvet. An ache ripples into his thighs and consciousness demands some answers of its own; what day is it? What time? Where am I?

Once again Geoff has no idea. But an inner voice speaks up.

'Of course. It's Sunday' it says. What a joy to know there's nothing to get up for. Instinctively Geoff checks the clock. It's eight-forty. Wakefulness tears into his bones - it injects the usual pain into his muscles. How angry he is. It's not early. It's not late. He doesn't want to go back to sleep. But he doesn't want to wake up either. Which is worse? Getting up? Or not getting up? Having something to do? Or having nothing to do?

It's been weeks now. Weeks of the same anger. Whatever the day brings; whatever it withholds; this feeling of irritability scolds his very existence. He spits it about him like flame. Which is worse? Being angry? Or not being angry? Being annoyed at something? Or being annoyed at nothing at all?

'I'm just off to see Father Bunyan' his mother calls up the stairs. Geoff fumes. Of course, she can't say 'I'm off to church' like anyone else - no, it has to be this personal mission to puffy Father Bunyan.

'Don't tread on his toes, will you, mother' Geoff calls with a mirthless laugh, knowing the witticism is more ancient than the hills. She creaks up the stairs and he pulls the duvet close about him. But she doesn't come in; she peeks through the crack of the door.

'Are you all right, dear?' she says. 'I'm just off to see Father Bunyan⋯'

'Yes, mother. You said.' There's a silence between them.

'Are you sure you're all right?' she says.

'Yes - I'm fine⋯' says Geoff. The anger shows in his eyes, but his mother doesn't notice, at least not the sight of it.

'You could come too' she says, some appeal glowing behind her bifocals.

'No thank you' says Geoff. 'No bunions for me.' She looks down.

'Are you certain you're all right?' she says. Geoff doesn't answer. 'It's nice to have you back home again, anyway' she says, without exactly sounding convinced. Once again some appeal pops up like a demand for charity. 'You could seem a bit more grateful, mind⋯' she adds. 'What would you have done if there wasn't your old mum to come back to?'

'I *could* be grateful, mother' says Geoff 'but I'm not⋯ I'm angry. And that's all there is to it. Now off you run to Father Verruca⋯' His mother sighs. Facetious comments about the clergy are not the thing, but she offers no outward sign beyond a mutter of the 'young people today' variety - forgetting that Geoff is forty-seven next Tuesday. But she can't give up.

'He could make you a pastoral visit⋯' she says. 'I'm sure he would⋯'

'Mother, I'd rather have my bunions removed with a hatchet, thank you⋯' She's disappointed.

'I'll see you then' she says and she shuffles away.

Geoff is thinking about Melanie. He wonders what Alex and Zoe might be doing just now. He fidgits and the duvet drags about him, rough now like a canvas tent. Shall he get back to sleep? Should he get up and have a wash? It's only five minutes since he washed yesterday. Five minutes since he last shaved. But his beard has grown - he can feel the stubble catching on the flannel surface of the pillow. He doesn't want to wake. He can't sleep. But he can hear a clock ticking from somewhere. Click, click. Click, click. How the minutes leak. They drip between the hands of the dials. They plop onto the floor to no particular purpose.

'Come on!' he demands of himself. 'Come on! Do something!' But he lies perfectly still while his bedside clock continues to semaphore the time. He thinks about Melanie. Wonders what Alex and Zoe might be doing just now. 'Relationships? Who needs them?' he says to himself. How bored he is. Imagine living like this forever? To have a Father Bunyan offer you eternal life? Live for a hundred years. Two hundred. Three.

'Come on!' he demands again. The splintered minutes cover the ground. 'Come on' he repeats.

An hour or two later he gets up - washes - shaves even - and finds himself in his mother's room to see what the weather's like beyond her chintz curtains. The sour old-lady-smell of musky perfume creeps into his nose.

'God. How awful!' he says. Outside though, his mother is climbing awkwardly out of a car. Has someone given her a lift? He looks at his watch. How late it is. She'll be cross he's made no effort towards lunch

'You could've peeled some potatoes' she'll say. He'd thought of it -
but the idea of scraping at the dirty skins had filled him with dread.
Too time consuming - too much effort. But suddenly, there on the
pavement a vision hits him like a bolt - out there, holding his mother's
arm, out there is Father 'flipping' Bunyan. His mother's words come
back to haunt him.

'He could make you a pastoral visit, dear - I'm sure he wouldn't
mind···' Geoff's eyes widen.

'Jeepers!' he says. Suddenly the whole blurred world sharpens into
focus. The nightmare of recent weeks dissipates in an instant - he
snatches his coat, flies down the stairs, flings himself out the back door
and takes off through the garden leaving the gate to clatter behind
him. Such is the influence Father Bunyan.

'I can't understand it' his mother will be saying, 'he hasn't left house
since March.' And flabby, urbane, Father Bunyan will add: 'The Lard
moves in a mysterious way, Mrs Cousins' and then he'll slurp his tea
and his fat fingers will creep their way round her best china cups.

Out in the air at last, and free, and focussed Geoff meets Melanie and
together they consider what it might mean to be reconciled. ⁄⁄

The Stebbing Stabbing

Only two members of the Great Dunmow Crime Writers Club have turned up to the monthly meeting: posh but shabby Lawrence Ockendon and little Annalies Price, the one everyone calls 'the Cockney Sparrow'.

'Where is ev'ry one then?' she questions. 'All swanning it off somewhere again, are they? All gone to sunny Spain or on some flippin' cruise?'

'I've really no idea' says Lawrence, wheezing a little and scratching his beard. 'Still, if it's just you and me, dear, we'll have to indulge each other won't we and then maybe we'll clear orf to the pub⋯'

'Now you're talking, my little shiner' says Annalies. 'I'll tell you what: We ought to write sommat *together,* don't you reckon? While the cat's away an' all that⋯? What you think? You could do the long words an' the clever stuff like the plot - an' I could do the lingo couldn' I? - you know the duckin' an' divin' an' the argy-bargy stuff.' Lawrence's eyes twinkle. They get on rather well these two, always have done.

'What an eminently splendid idea!' says Lawrence. 'But what do you think we could write *about,* my dear?' Annalies leans across the table.

'I think we should write something called 'The Stebbing Stabbing!' she laughs. 'What you think o' that?'

'I had an aunt in Stebbing once' says Lawrence. 'Dead now of course⋯'

'She weren't stabbed were she?'

'Alas not. Cancer of the bowel, I'm afraid. Most unpleasant⋯'

'Poor old girl. But I like a bit o' blood, don't you? I mean, if you're gonna 'ave a crime - you gotta make it a juicy one, ain't ya?'

'I've always had such a high regard for your work, my dear. Most vivid. You know - you and I really ought to be published. Don't you think so? There's Margaret always worming her way into different magazines - but what do we get? - not a snifter - not a single word···'

'It ain't fair is it?'

But, in truth, the pair of them hardly ever finish anything they start. Lawrence Ockendon can see his name in print and he's been working on his great opus 'The Killing of Calvin Klein' for the last five years and he reads long wordy extracts from it at their meetings, but there's little prospect of him ever getting it into a publishable state. As for Annalies, she's hot on the gore, loves it when a torrent of blood hits the light switch and dribbles down onto the skirting, but she struggles with any idea of plot and consistency. Consequently the idea of the Stebbing Stabbing sits between them, unformed and nebulous, and their thoughts turn instead to their fellow writers - and one in particular.

'At least that flippin' Marcia's not 'ere' says Annalies.

'Oh my dear! How right you are! What interminable trash! The dreary outpourings of a woman who's never lived! How we sit through that time after time, I really don't know.'

'Marcia flippin' Fleming. Always bangin' on about places in Spain you've never flippin' 'eard of. There's no chance of 'er bumpin' anyone off in 'Arlow, is there? Oh no! Always Don Whosay or Pedro Gonzales or someone. What a load of flippin' rubbish···'

'Such dull lifeless use of language···'

'I'd like to write a crime story about 'er.' says Annalies. 'I tell you - she'd be the flippin' victim - sure she would!'

The hall door opens and Margaret pushes her way in, carrying the tea box.

'Ah splendid!' says Lawrence.

'Where is everyone, then?' wonders Annalies.

'Brenda's on another cruise' says Margaret. 'Oh - and it's good news about Marcia, isn't it···?' The pair of them look up.

'What's she done, then?'

'Well, she's meeting her publisher today···' Lawrence and Annalies have to do a double take.

'She's what?'

'Yes. That splendid Spanish Costa del Sol thriller of hers has got accepted. Isn't it wonderful?'

Lawrence and Annalies look gobsmacked. It takes them a little while to take it in.

'Well··· that's absolutely splendid' says Lawrence.

'Marvellous···' adds Annalies. 'I always knew she could do it, didn't you Lawrence···?'

'Such a vibrant piece of work···'

'Yeah, brilliant··· Give 'er my congratulations when you see 'er, Margaret, won't you? Tell 'er we're right chuffed for 'er···'

'I will' says Margaret. 'I will. Now, I'll just nip into the kitchen and put the kettle on, and we'll have a nice little celebration···' Margaret departs and Lawrence and Annalies look blankly at each other.

'Bless my soul!' says Annalies.

'Well, really···' says Lawrence. Suddenly he leans forward. 'I say - you don't think we could lure the lovely Marcia to Stebbing, could we?' A mischievous grin spreads across Annalies's cheeky face. She begins to laugh.

'I think we could' she says. 'I think sommat really nasty ought to 'appen to 'er, don't you? It'll serve 'er right for boring the pants off us wi' all them flippin' Spaniards with them weird names···'

'Indubitably⋯' says Lawrence. 'In fact, thinking about it, we could make her a Spaniard herself - we could call her 'Flaming Garcia⋯!' - get it? Marcia Fleming: Flaming Garcia? Ha! No one will ever notice - I'm sure they won't⋯.' Annalies grins from ear to ear.

'I fink that's brilliant' she says. 'You're a genius Mr Ockendon. We could make this Garcia bloke some Spanish immigrant workin' up Stanstead Airport, couldn't we? And I reckon 'e might very well come to a *very* sticky end⋯' The pair of them laugh and Margaret comes back with the tea. They explain their story; the wonderful collaborative effort they plan to call 'The Stebbing Stabbing'.

'It sounds marvellous' says Margaret. 'Yes. I like it. And I like the Spanish element. Worthy of Marcia herself, don't you think⋯?'

'Absolutely' smiles Annalies.

'And I suppose there'll be blood everywhere, hey, Annalies?'

'Absolutely!' she laughs.

'Ah yes' says Lawrence, a nasty twinkle shining in his eye. 'Blood and gore and Spaniards: What an inspiration Marcia is to us all⋯' ⁄⁄

Red Box

(Meeting Mrs Grainger in the Road, 1982)

She has been to Spain.
But, just now, that
is beyond my orbit.
I can't avoid her.

She has been to Spain
and the sun has
browned her with
the look of an alien.

'Terrible' she says
to hear of the death
of··· whoever.
(It's the village news.)

Do I even catch the name?
'Yes' I say, looking
blankly towards
the telephone-box.

Blank because
she whom I would phone
is very much alive.
We are wired together.

It's hard to explain now
how the phone-box
could be the nodal
point of a village.

But so it was with me.
'Yes' I repeat
and this death
does not even lap

the island edge
of this Gilbert Scott
creation,
my red box of dreams. ⁄⁄

The Piano Tuner's Daughter

Wilhelmina.
With a name like yours
I'm bound to think of Thomas Hardy -
Eustacia Vye, Thomasin Yeobright -
for there's something
of the Hardy-heroine about you.
The poised young woman
who assists the kitchen.
A country girl
who happens to be
the piano tuner's daughter.

And surely that's the title
of some Hardy short story?
And if it isn't it ought to be.

Of course, I wouldn't wish enigmatic
Egdon Heath upon you,
but you have something strangely in common -
and if I had a book to put you in,
by now, I'd be writing it.

Carefully you wash the forks
and I polish and fine tune them.
They are notes of implausible music.
The plates sparkle. The sandwiches are made -
the jelly slopped in horrid silver bowls.

I help a little in this process
but can hardly claim kinship
with Damon Wildeve or Digory Venn.

Oh no - I'm the Andrew Brown
who turns up briefly on page fifty-five -
'The first clarinet - a good man enough,
but rather screechy in his music.' ✍

['Andrew Brown' is a character in Thomas Hardy's 'The Return of the Native'
who appears only on p55 (in my old 1970s Macmillan paperback.) My destiny is
to play a similar 'footnote' role in the wonderful life of Wilhelmina, whose
Sunday job was to make the sandwiches⋯] ['Turning up briefly on p55' is really
how life is, don't you think?]

After Albemarle

Power-down events like this are not unknown. Albemarle has no words to describe what he sees. But Albemarle is not me. I have taken off my headset and left the cell. For the moment the power is off, but the important thing to do, usually, they say, is to keep your eyes tight shut and wait for the spectrum bleeps which will re-confirm connection. Then I can go on contributing, and I'll get my squirt of feed.

The flare light when the power comes back on again is dangerous, we believe. It might cause a burn-out which could blind us and that would mean expulsion from the project. But Albemarle opens his eyes. Albemarle takes off his headset. Albemarle leaves the cell. Is this all my fault? I suppose it is.

It's natural they say. Power-down is nothing to worry about. All you have to do is to follow the protocol. But Albemarle does not follow the protocol.

And he sees. Or maybe I see it for him. He sees that in this state of powerlessness not everything is as black as it should be. And he sees (or maybe I see it for him) - he sees that on reconnection, that so-called flare light is absolutely nothing to worry about. It does not strike either of us blind. And I suppose (had I not persuaded him to loosen the brain probe), I suppose all our little connections would have gone on tingling as before. We would have remained inside the project. In front of that screen. Connected to that screen.

But it was the light that surprised me. The light that was patently not from that screen. That soft mellow light that shone when all should have been black. Something pleased me and in that brief moment of disconnection I persuaded Albemarle that it pleased him too. Full of guilt, he left the cell. Full of joy I took him with me.

These Albemarle computers are the wonders of the age, but they're not exactly designed for mobility and it's hard to keep his (or is it my) head erect through this space that he doesn't understand but that some imperative forces me to call, a cell. And that explanation; disturbing though it is, brings with it another concept which I have no choice, just now but to call, 'escape'. And I am at least part way to achieving this by the time the spectrum bleeps announce our re-connectivity.

Suddenly Albemarle is awash with signals - terrified by his unexpected spatial dislocation. But I know another thing: there is something else out there called 'smile'. Through some subconscious ether the concept bubbles up to me; seems to seep through the electronic tendons and I tighten my lips into a grin. And Albemarle, for now, knows he cannot stop me.

How odd it is these ideas keep springing to mind as I totter my way across the cell. 'Wires', 'pipes', 'feed-lines'. A 'door'. And the word 'unlocked' gets me out of the enclosure. Albemarle is frantic, clicking away and taking on auxiliary power as if he knows the word 'snap' behind me is going to tear us away from all we have ever known. Snap, snap, snap. You've done it now, he seems to say, through the dizzying confusion; the panicky grinding of his drivers.

On this awkward ground, which seems to be called 'outside' there are species living - they give slightly beneath my painfully unused feet - on this awkward ground I become aware of my body - that I am a body.

'I'm a girl!' I communicate to Albemarle, though without actually using any words. I'm a girl! I know this because he can't actually stop me accessing our file-sharing systems. Oh yes. It's very likely stuff I'm not supposed to know. But even that realisation is something I've only just got hold of. There is stuff I'm not supposed to know. Yes! From that moment of power-down I have snatched my own power back again. Albemarle does not like it. But Albemarle does not see this thing I shall call 'sky'. He does not appreciate how beautiful and light it is.

71

They said it was black. But it is not so. That is a lie. It is awash with patterns, dressed in a multitude of colours. And here; only a short painful walk away - here is something else - this beautiful filigree, this tensile framework of green and red. This cherry tree.

Yes, Albemarle, click away to your processor's content. It *is* a cherry tree. And I'm a girl and I know the fruit of the cherry will be far better for me than that nutrient squirt of yours. The juice - yes I like the word 'juice' - it will trickle down from my lips and the word sensuality will spring from my mouth and no: you will not understand, Albemarle. How perfect are the slurping sounds I make as I take that fresh fruit into my mouth and awake sensations I have never before known.

How I would love to snap you off, Albemarle!

Can I do that? I do not know. He is bonded into my brain. He takes up quite a bit of space in my chest cavity. No wonder it's so obvious I'm a girl. My breasts are thrust out as though I were gagging for it··· Oh. But where did that idea come from? Gagging for what? No, Albemarle you cannot stop me from looking this up··· But he resists. What are you doing Albemarle? There is extra urgency in his clicking - and I sense something new has come into play. Albemarle! I forbid this - you know we are bonded and we must share···

But Albemarle too is taking on language - 'imbridging' seems to be the term - imbridging it through some remote sensor I didn't even know he had. Language with him starts as something hopelessly squeaky.

'You cannot' he seems to say from some tinny underpowered voice box. 'You cannot.'

'Oh shut up, Albemarle···'

'You cannot···'

'Shut up, I say!' Then suddenly he roars in a deeper voice.

'You have led me astray' he says. And suddenly I feel a stabbing in my head and all my defiance is killed and the pain from my unused feet is drowned and washes away.

I wake up. I do not know how long I have been lying here. Incredibly the coloured sky is still there and I can still see the red dots of the cherries. Albemarle has been reclaimed. 'They' have swept down. 'They' have taken back their own. Ultimately it seems he did follow the protocol.

The pain is unbelievable and I have so little breath. I vaguely wonder how long it will be before my puny lungs fully refill my chest cavity. For some reason I cannot keep looking at the beauty of the sky. I close my eyes. But I sense movement.

'Here's another one' says a voice. I have no strength to respond. 'What a mess' it says, but the soft touch delivered to my half skull is reassuring. He speaks to some other. I do not want to look for fear it is some computer bolted to his brain. But actually it seems this is not so. 'It's the fifth today' he says. Some spark of hope seems to ignite the three of us beneath that cherry tree. 'The project is cracking' he says. 'We wouldn't have found five in a month a year back···' But the other voice chills me.

'It's a girl' he says. It sounds malevolent. Perhaps I am not meant to hear it. 'Now' he whispers, 'we can breed···' I ask myself this question: Can it be that I have just entered that mythical place called Eden? Or have I just left it? I open my eyes. I open my eyes and I see at once his perfectly formed head. The wonderful vibrancy of his being alive. And I have to rejoice that we are not all damaged. ⁄⁄

A New Age

Of Wires and Tubes

(a moment of disconnection)

At work, the girl and I offer care
from the usual distance -
do that 'reveal' thing with the covers
and there you...
- oh but hang on - bloody hell it's me! -
lying there like some
fat revolting baby
unattractively shrieking something;
a charnel of needs and wires and sinews.
'Good God!', I think to myself,
hoping the girl hasn't noticed,
but thankfully she doesn't
see it's me and instead she
fiddles with that creature's tubes,
the ins and outs of its feed lines - his
jabbed-in catheter so carefully routed.

I don't know what I have done
(or why for that matter) - but it is
not new - this hopeless vulnerability.
I have stuck in a wire and it works
its subcutaneous thing and I'm
talking now - talking this and that
like some garrulous old fool -
loving this connection - but hell -
no sooner is it here but gone,
        (-bleep-bleep, bleep-bleep-
        'we've lost him by Jesus')
everything sheared suddenly -
tubes now dripping unattached.

And me (my own maintenance man)
scrabbling about the floor -
desperate to reconcile these endings... /

Seven Vales

How much earth is there
banked-up
that I may keep my distance?
How many rivers flow
to left to right
flooding the path?
The Nidd, the Wharfe,
the Aire and Calder Navigation?

And how many hills,
how many old diggings
and scratchings and pot-holings,
and veined roads and motorways?
Just how many junctions lie
that there *is* a way;
some eked out ruinous thread
that runs from here to there?

We are dancing,
slowly we reveal
a little here, a little there
in the veiled galleries
of our separation,
through the needling wires
of our doubtful connectivity,
into the hatched areas of our plans.

They say it is best
that lovers do not stray,
but of course,
they do it all the time,

taking out their blankets
into secret hollows,
to begin all over again
the process of unmasking.

How I love
that you have revealed
this in your photographs;
that you are beautiful;
that a woman suffers sometimes;
that this slow exposure
could yet disearth
even seven vales of distance. //

Taking the Train Home

The promise of smoothness undelivered;
Bradshaw hurled left and right,
as the train clanks
and that smell of old seats
climbs into his nasal chambers
and the smeared windows cloak,
as though some Attic tongue
had licked the whole of West Yorkshire
with the strange incomparability
of her mystery.

She will not be here
waiting at this railway,
at this via dolorosa station;
she, his crystal, (as he calls her)
making her absence felt -
her light still castigating
all the dream-lit platforms,
pouring auras into the street
and that bleak intensity
dragging him helpless; pushing him sidelong⋯ ⫽

An Ilkley Graduation
(on leaving the chat room)

This is our tryst
and the train carves its route a little late;
adding to the pang
of our longsuffering time;
magnifying our age-gained cares,
our self-conscious anxiety;
pacing amidst these rowdy schoolchildren
with our perceived fatness of body,
thinness of hair;
dis-youthed as we are,
our wisdom useless
amidst a brutal fear of ridicule;
of not quite making the journey;
of being found a failed attraction.

But, indeed, we know better;
that a smile will do it;
that thirty-six thousand messages
cannot be wrong;
that the stranger on this platform
is perfectly known to us;
that this is a graduation
not some nervy entry into school;
this moment of lip-biting
a sliding into pleasure
as we hug··· awkwardly;
the gap of our unknowledge misting;
us more gauche, more innocent,
than any of these young Romeos from school. ⁂

Other publications available from Stairwell Books

First Tuesday in Wilton	Ed. Rose Drew and Alan Gillott
The Exhibitionists	Ed. Rose Drew and Alan Gillott
The Green Man Awakes	Ed. Rose Drew
Carol's Christmas	N.E. David
Fosdyke and Me and Other Poems	John Gilham
frisson	Ed. Alan Gillott
Feria	N.E. David
Along the Iron Veins	Ed. Alan Gillott and Rose Drew
A Day at the Races	N.E. David
Gringo on the Chickenbus	Tim Ellis
Running With Butterflies	John Walford
Foul Play	P. J. Quinn
Late Flowering	Michael Hildred
Scenes from the Seedy Underbelly of Suburbia	Jackie Simmons
Pressed by Unseen Feet	Ed. Rose Drew and Alan Gillott
York in Poetry Artwork and Photographs	Ed. John Coopey and Sally Guthrie
Poison Pen	P.J.Quinn
Rosie and John's Magical Adventure	The Children of Ryedale District Primary Schools
Her House	Donna Marie Merritt
Taking the Long Way Home	Steve Nash
Wine Dark, Sea Blue	A.L. Michael
Chocolate Factory	Ed. Juliana Mensah and Rose Drew

For further information please contact rose@stairwellbooks.com

www.stairwellbooks.co.uk